People Around Town / Gente de mi ciudad

MEET THE TEACHER/ TE PRESENTO A LOS MAESTROS

I0868290

By Joyce Jeffries

Traducción al español: Eduardo Alamán

Gareth Stevens Publishing

Please visit our website, www.garethstevens.com. For a free color catalog of all our high-quality books, call toll free 1-800-542-2595 or fax 1-877-542-2596.

Library of Congress Cataloging-in-Publication Data

Jeffries, Joyce, author.
[Meet the teacher. Spanish]
Meet the teacher = Te presento a los maestros / Joyce Jeffries.
pages cm. — (People around town = Gente de mi ciudad)
Includes index.
In English and Spanish.
ISBN 978-1-4339-7392-5 (library binding)
1. Teachers—Juvenile literature. I. Jeffries, Joyce, author. Meet the teacher. English. II. Title. III. Title: Te presento a los maestros.
LB1775.J4418 2013
371.1—dc23

2012012855

First Edition

Published in 2013 by
Gareth Stevens Publishing
111 East 14th Street, Suite 349
New York, NY 10003

Editor: Katie Kawa
Designer: Andrea Davison-Bartolotta
Spanish Translation: Eduardo Alamán

Photo credits: Cover, pp. 13, 19, 24 (library) Digital Vision/Thinkstock; p. 1 Hemera/Thinkstock; p. 5 iStockphoto/Thinkstock; p. 7 Brand X Pictures/Thinkstock; pp. 9, 24 (pencil) Juriah Mosin/Shutterstock.com; p. 11 Creatas/Thinkstock; pp. 15, 17, 24 (chalkboards) Photodisc/Thinkstock; p. 21 Nadejda Ivanova/Shutterstock.com; p. 23 Wavebreak Media/Thinkstock.

Printed in the United States of America

CPSIA compliance information: Batch #CS12GS: For further information contact Gareth Stevens, New York, New York at 1-800-542-2595.

Contents

Contenido

A teacher works
with a group of kids.
This is her class.

Los maestros trabajan
con un grupo de niños.
Esta es su clase.

She helps them write new words.

La maestra les ayuda a escribir nuevas palabras.

They write with pencils.

Los chicos escriben con lápices.

She helps them read books too.

Los maestros también les ayudan a leer.

They go to a place with a lot of books. This is a library.

Los maestros van a un lugar en donde hay muchos libros. Esta es la biblioteca.

DICTIONARY

Teachers use maps. These show different places on Earth.

Los maestros usan mapas. Los mapas muestran diferentes lugares de la Tierra.

They write on boards. These are called chalkboards.

Los maestros escriben en lugares especiales. Estos lugares se llaman pizarras.

apple
ant
atom
airplane

There are many kinds of teachers.

Hay muchos tipos de maestros.

Anthony
Jake
Sabrina
Roy
Charles

Some teach about the past. This is called history.

Algunos maestros enseñan acerca del pasado. A esto se le llama historia.

Some teach math.
They help kids add.

Algunos maestros enseñan matemáticas. Los maestros ayudan a los niños a sumar.

2+1=3
2+2=4
2+3=5

Words to Know/ Palabras que debes saber

chalkboard/
(la) pizarra

library/
(la) biblioteca

pencil/
(el) lápiz

Index / Índice